Identity Theft:
A Comprehensive Guide

Identity Theft:
A Comprehensive Guide

Jay Mason

iUniverse, Inc.
New York Lincoln Shanghai

Identity Theft: A Comprehensive Guide

iUniverse books may be ordered through booksellers or by contacting:

iUniverse
2021 Pine Lake Road, Suite 100
Lincoln, NE 68512
www.iuniverse.com
1-800-Authors (1-800-288-4677)

Because of the dynamic nature of the Internet, any Web addresses or links contained in this book may have changed since publication and may no longer be valid.

The views expressed in this work are solely those of the author and do not necessarily reflect the views of the publisher, and the publisher hereby disclaims any responsibility for them.

ISBN: 978-0-595-48128-6 (pbk)
ISBN: 978-0-595-60226-1 (ebk)

Printed in the United States of America

A special thanks to Ann Dieleman for your leadership, support and editing skills.

Thank you to Dell Kubler for your support and Foreword.

For Marigene, the love of my life, and for Jack, Max and Abby.

Press On

Nothing in this world can take the place of persistence.

Talent will not; nothing is more common than unsuccessful men with talent.

Genius will not; unrewarded genius is almost a proverb.

Education alone will not; the world is full of educated derelicts.

Persistence and determination alone are omnipotent.

—Calvin Coolidge, 30th President of the United States

Contents

Foreword

Identity theft is scary. Clever ads on television shock our imagination into full bloom. We hear fear-based ads on the radio and we listen to horror stories shared with us by relatives and neighbors. Who are these thieves? How do they find us? What do they do in our name? Where are they hiding?

Identity theft leads to collection notices and ruined credit. Our friends and neighbors describe months if not years of telephone calls and endless paperwork needed to clear their good name with credit bureaus and mistaken creditors. If we dig a little deeper we hear of lawsuits and even incarceration as the result of misused and stolen identities.

Most of us have plenty of our own debt to manage. We certainly don't need the nightmare of false debt added by criminals who strike at us from unseen places like ghosts in the night. In an ever advancing technological society, the real threat of having our identities stolen gets worse, never better. The truth of the matter is that it is easier for a criminal to steal your identity than to create one from scratch.

But where do we go for help? How many of us truly understand how this crime is committed, how to prevent the crime from happening to us, or how to recover should we become a victim?

Jay Mason brings this national crisis into clear focus with this timely and educational book. Identity Theft: A Comprehensive Guide, identifies how thieves accomplish their crime, what they do with your information, 40 ways to prevent the crime, and full recovery solutions.

As important as Identity Theft: A Comprehensive Guide is for you as an individual, it is equally, if not more, important for employer groups. The damage this crime is causing in the workplace is unmeasurably destructive. Loss time from work, presenteeism, stress on personal budgets, and legal issues from debt collection matters all pull from the productive time of your best employees. New Federal criminal codes regarding cyber crime negligence put the employer at new and more severe legal risk.

One of the fastest growing areas of identity theft is in the medical records arena. More and more personal medical records are being compromised to provide criminals with instantly new identities with available medical insurance coverage. Any employer is at risk in these situations of having their health care and other employee benefit experience negatively effected and accelerating the rising cost of health care beyond its natural trend.

If you want to protect yourself, or if you want to protect your business, Jay Mason's timely book Identity Theft: A Comprehensive Guide, is a prudent if not necessary purchase.

Dell Kubler is the Vice President of Swerdlin Benefits Company in Atlanta, Georgia. As a Certified Identity Theft Risk Manager, Dell has worked on a national basis to help protect individuals and businesses from the growing threat of identity theft for the past 8 years.

1

The Crime of Identity Theft

In the course of a busy day you may buy gas, write a check for school activities, retrieve cash from an ATM, buy groceries, rent a car, mail your tax returns, or apply for a credit card. Chances are you don't give these everyday transactions a second thought. But an identity thief does.

Identity theft is a serious crime. People whose identities have been stolen can spend years and thousands of dollars cleaning up the mess the thieves have made of a good name and credit record. In the meantime, victims of identity theft may lose job opportunities, be refused loans for education, housing, or cars, and even get arrested for crimes they did not commit. Humiliation, anger, and frustration are among the feelings victims experience as they navigate the process of rescuing their identity.

It Can Happen To Anyone

The crime of identity theft is on the rise and, according to the Federal Trade Commission, it is the fastest growing crime in the U.S. Recent surveys show there are currently about 11 million new victims each year. Identity thieves routinely steal Social Security Numbers, dates of birth, driver's licenses, credit card numbers, ATM cards, telephone calling cards, health insurance cards, and other pieces of individuals' identities such as PIN numbers and even your mother's maiden name. They use this information to impersonate their victims and to spend as much money as they can in as short a time as possible before moving on to someone else.

Victims are left with a tainted reputation and the complicated task of restoring their good names.

There Are Five Main Types of Identity Theft

1. Financial Identity Theft—This type of case typically focuses on your name and Social Security number. The identity thief may apply for telephone service, credit cards or loans, buy merchandise, or lease cars or apartments.

2. Criminal Identity Theft—The imposter in this crime provides the victim's information instead of his or her own when stopped by law enforcement. Eventually, when the warrant for arrest is issued, it is in the name of the person issued the citation—you.

3. Identity Cloning—In this crime, the thief uses your information to establish a new life and they work and live as you. Examples include illegal aliens, criminals avoiding warrants, people hiding from abusive situations, or actually becoming a "new person" to leave behind a poor work and financial history.

4. Business or Commercial Identity Theft—Businesses are also victims of identity theft. Typically, the perpetrator gets credit cards or checking accounts in the name of the business. The business finds out when suppliers send collection notices or when their business credit rating score is affected.

5. Medical Identity Theft—This occurs when the victim's medical insurance identity is stolen to obtain health care. The most valuable piece of information in most people's wallet is their medical insurance card that typically has a limit approaching $1 million or more in potential benefits.

No matter what type of identity theft is involved, the result is a long and arduous road to recovery. As in all crimes, preventing the crime from occurring in the first place is paramount.

There Are Two Main Ways in Which Identity Theft Can Occur

- "Account takeover" occurs when a thief acquires your existing credit account information and purchases products and services using either the actual credit card or the account number and expiration date.

- "Application fraud" occurs with an identity thief uses your social security number and other identifying information to open new accounts in your name. Victims are not likely to learn of application fraud for some time because the monthly account statements are mailed to an address used by the imposter. Victims learn of account takeovers when they receive their monthly account statement.

Generally, victims of credit card fraud are liable for no more than the first $50 of the loss. In most cases the victim will not be required to pay any part of the loss, but debit card users have less protection against fraud. Not only are individuals' checking accounts wiped out, but debit card users could be liable for the total amount of the loss depending on how quickly they report the loss to their financial institution.

Even though victims are usually not responsible for paying their imposters bills, they are often left with a bad credit report and must spend months and even years regaining their financial health. In the meantime, they have difficulty getting credit, obtaining loans, renting apartments, and even getting hired. Victims of identity theft find little help from the authorities as they attempt to untangle the web of deception that has allowed another person to impersonate them.

Despite your best efforts to manage the flow of your personal information or to keep it to yourself, skilled identity thieves may use a variety of methods to gain access to your data.

How Identity Thieves Get Your Personal Information

- They may steal your mail, including bank and credit card statements, credit card offers, new checks, and tax information.

- They may rummage through your trash, the trash of businesses, or public trash dumps in a practice known as "dumpster diving."

- They may get your credit reports by abusing authorized access or by posing as a landlord, employer, or someone else who may have a right to access your report.

- They may steal your credit or debit card numbers by capturing the information in a data storage device in a practice known as "skimming." They may swipe your card for an actual purchase or attach the device to an ATM where you may enter or swipe your card.

- They may steal your wallet or purse.

- They may complete a "change of address form" to divert your mail to another location.

- They may steal personal information they find in your home.

- They may steal information from you through email or phone by posing as legitimate companies and claiming that you have a problem with your account. This practice is known as "phishing" online, or "pretexting" by phone.

How Identity Thieves Use Your Personal Information:

- Thieves may call your credit card issuer to change the billing address on your credit card account. The imposter then runs up charges on your account. Because your bills are being sent to a different address, it may be some time before you realize there's a problem.

- They may open new credit card accounts in your name. When they use the credit cards and don't pay the bills, the delinquent accounts are reported on your credit report.

- Imposters may establish phone or wireless service in your name.

- They may open a bank account in your name and write bad checks on that account.

- Counterfeit checks or credit or debit cards can be made, or thieves can authorize electronic transfers in your name and drain your bank account.

- Thieves may file for bankruptcy under your name to avoid paying debts they've incurred under your name or to avoid eviction.

- They may buy a car by taking out an auto loan in your name.

- Identification such as a driver's license issued with their picture in your name may be obtained.

- They may get a job or file fraudulent tax returns in your name.

- Your name may be given to the police during an arrest. If they don't show up for their court date, a warrant for arrest is issued in your name.

Misuse of Personal Information

- On average, 49% of victims did not know how their information was obtained.

- 26% reported that they were alerted to suspicious account activity by companies such as credit card issuers or banks.

- 8% reported that they first learned of the identity theft when they applied for credit and were turned down.

- 15% of all victims reported that their personal information was misused in non-financial ways—to obtain government documents, for example—or on tax forms.

- 67% of identity theft victims reported that existing credit card accounts were misused.

- 19% reported that checking or savings accounts were misused.

- Nearly one-quarter of all victims said their information was lost or stolen, including lost or stolen credit cards, checkbooks or social security cards.

- Stolen mail was the source of information for identity thieves in four percent of all victims.

FTC, 2005 Consumer Fraud and Identity Theft Complaint Data, January 2006

- The most common forms of identity theft

  - Credit card fraud (26%)

  - Phone or utilities fraud (18%)

  - Bank fraud (17%)

  - Employment fraud (12%)

  - Government documents/benefits fraud (9%)

  - Loan fraud (5%)

2

Free Annual Credit Report

The Fair Credit Reporting Act (FCRA) requires each of the three nationwide consumer reporting companies—Equifax, Experian, and TransUnion—to provide you with a free copy of your credit report, at your request, once every 12 months. FCRA also promotes the accuracy and privacy of information in the files of the nation's consumer reporting companies. The Federal Trade Commission (FTC), the nation's consumer protection agency, enforces the FCRA with respect to consumer reporting companies.

A credit report includes information on where you live, how you pay your bills, and whether you've been sued, arrested, or filed for bankruptcy. Nationwide consumer reporting companies sell the information in your report to creditors, insurers, employers, and other businesses that use it to evaluate your applications for credit, insurance, employment, or renting a home.

The three nationwide consumer reporting companies have set up a central website, a toll-free telephone number, and a mailing address through which you can order your free annual report.

To order your free report, visit www.annualcreditreport.com, call 1-877-322-8228, or complete the Annual Credit Report Request Form from www.ftc.gov/credit. Do not contact the three nationwide consumer reporting companies individually.

You may order your reports from each of the three nationwide consumer reporting companies at the same time or you can order your report from each of the organizations one at a time. The law allows you to order one free copy of your report from each of the nationwide consumer reporting companies once every 12 months.

A Warning About "Imposter" Websites

Only one website is authorized to fill orders for the free annual credit report you are entitled to under law—www.annualcreditreport.com. Other websites that claim to offer "free credit reports," "free credit scores," or "free credit monitoring" are not part of the free annual credit report program. In some cases, the "free" product comes with strings attached. For example, some sites sign you up for a supposedly "free" service that converts to one you have to pay for after a trial period. If you don't cancel during the trial period you may be agreeing to let the company start charging fees to your credit card.

Some imposter sites use terms like "free report" in their names and others have URLs that purposely misspell annualcreditreport.com in the hope that you will mistype the name of the official site. Some of these imposter sites direct you to other sites that try to sell you something or collect your personal information.

Annualcreditreport.com and the nationwide consumer reporting companies will not send you an email asking for your personal information. If you get an email, see a pop-up ad, or get a phone call from someone claiming to be from annualcreditreport.com or any of the three nationwide consumer reporting companies, do not reply or click on any link in the message.

Requesting Your Report

To receive your report you need to provide your name, address, Social Security number, and date of birth. If you have moved in the last two years you may have to provide your previous address. To maintain the security of your file, each nationwide consumer reporting company may ask you for some information that only you would know like the amount of your monthly mortgage payment. Each company may ask you for different information because the information each has in your file may come from different sources.

If you request your report online at annualcreditreport.com you should be able to access it immediately. If you order your report by calling 1-877-322-8228, your report will be processed and mailed to you within 15 days. If you order your report by mail using the Annual Credit Report Request Form, your request will be processed and mailed to you within 15 days of receipt.

Whether you order your report online, by phone, or by mail, it may take longer to receive your report if the nationwide consumer reporting company needs more information to verify your identity.

Under federal law you are entitled to a free report if a company takes adverse action against you such as denying your application for credit, insurance, or employment and you ask for your report within 60 days of receiving notice of the action. The notice will give you the name, address, and phone number of the consumer reporting company. You are also entitled to one free report a year if you are unemployed and plan to look for a job within 60 days, if you are on welfare, or if your report is inaccurate because of fraud, including identity theft. Otherwise, a consumer reporting company may charge you up to $9.50 for another copy of your report within a 12-month period.

Under FCRA, both the consumer reporting company and the information provider (that is, the person, company, or organization that provides information about you to a consumer reporting company) are responsible for correcting inaccurate or incomplete information in your report. To take full advantage of your rights under this law, contact the consumer reporting company and the information provider.

Tell the consumer reporting company, in writing, what information you think is inaccurate. Consumer reporting companies must investigate the items in question unless they consider your dispute frivolous. They also must forward all the relevant data you provide about the inaccuracy to the organization that provided the information. After the information provider receives notice of a dispute from the consumer reporting company, it must investigate, review the relevant information, and report the results back to the consumer reporting company. If the information provider finds the disputed information is inaccurate, it must notify all three nationwide consumer reporting companies so they can correct the information in your file.

When the investigation is complete the consumer reporting company must give you the written results and a free copy of your report if the dispute results in a change. If an item is changed or deleted the consumer reporting company cannot put the disputed information back in your file unless the information provider verifies that it is accurate and complete. The consumer reporting company also must send you written notice that includes the name, address, and phone number of the information provider.

If an investigation doesn't resolve your dispute with the consumer reporting company you can ask that a statement of the dispute be included in your file and in future reports. You can also ask the consumer reporting company to provide your statement to anyone who received a copy of your report in the recent past.

If you tell the information provider that you dispute an item, a notice of your dispute must be included any time the information provider reports the item to a consumer reporting company.

A consumer reporting company can report most accurate negative information for seven years and bankruptcy information for 10 years. There is no time limit on reporting information about criminal convictions, information reported in response to your application for a job that pays more than $75,000 per year, and information reported because you've applied for more than $150,000 worth of credit or life insurance. Information about a lawsuit or an unpaid judgment against you can be reported for seven years or until the statute of limitations runs out, whichever is longer.

FCRA specifies who can access your credit report. Creditors, insurers, employers, and other businesses that use the information in your report to evaluate your applications for credit, insurance, employment, or renting a home are among those that have a legal right to access your report.

Your employer can obtain a copy of your credit report only if you agree. A consumer reporting company may not provide information about you to your employer, or to a prospective employer, without your written consent.

3

"Phishing" Scams

"Phishing" involves the use of fraudulent emails and copy-cat websites to trick you into revealing valuable personal information such as your account numbers for banking, securities, mortgage, or credit accounts, your social security number, and the login IDs and passwords you use when accessing online financial services providers. The fraudsters who collect this information then use it to steal your money, your identity or both.

When identity thieves go on phishing expeditions, they lure their targets into a false sense of security by using the familiar, trusted logos of established, legitimate companies. A typical phishing scam starts with sending out millions of emails that appear to come from a high-profile financial services provider or a respected Internet auction house.

The email will usually ask you to provide information about yourself or to verify information that you previously provided when you established your online account. To maximize the chances that a recipient will respond, the thief might employ any or all of the following tactics:

- Names of Real Companies—Rather than create from scratch a phony company, the fraudster might use a legitimate company's name and incorporate the look and feel of its website—including the color scheme and graphics—into the phishy email.

- "From" an Actual Employee—The "from" line or the text of the message (or both) might contain the names of real people who actually work for the company. That way, if you contacted the company to confirm whether "Jane Doe" truly is vice president of client services, you would get a positive response and feel assured.

- URLs that Appear Correct—The email might include a convenient link to a seemingly legitimate website where you can enter the information the thief wants to steal. In reality, though, the website will be a "spoofed" website that looks like the real thing. In some cases the link might lead to select pages of a legitimate website such as the real company's actual privacy policy or legal disclaimer.

- Urgent Messages—Many identity thieves use fear to trigger a response and phishers are no different. In common phishing scams the emails warn that failure to respond will result in you no longer having access to your account. Other emails might claim that the company has detected suspicious activity in your account or that it is implementing new privacy software or identity theft solutions.

How to Protect Yourself from Phishing

The best way you can protect yourself from phishers is to understand what legitimate financial service providers and respectable online auction houses will and will not do. Most importantly, legitimate entities will not ask you to provide or verify sensitive information through a non-secure means such as email.

Follow these five steps to protect yourself from phishers:

1. Pick Up the Phone to Verify—Do not respond to any emails that request personal or financial information, especially ones that use pressure tactics or prey on fear. If you have reason to believe that a financial institution actually does need personal information from you, call the company yourself using the number in your account information rather than the one the email provides.

2. Do Your Own Typing—Rather than merely clicking on the link provided in the email, type the URL into your web browser yourself. Even though a URL in an email may look legitimate, fraudsters can mask the true destination.

3. Beef Up Your Security—Personal firewalls and security software packages (with anti-virus, anti-spam, and spyware detection features) are a must-have if you engage in online financial transactions. Make sure your computer has the latest security patches and make sure that you conduct your financial transactions only on a secure web page using encryption. You can tell if a page is secure in a couple of ways. Look for a closed

padlock in the status bar and see that the URL starts with "https" instead of just "http."

Some phishers make spoofed websites which appear to have padlocks. To double-check, click on the padlock icon on the status bar to see the security certificate for the site. Following the "Issued to" in the pop-up window you should see the name matching the site you think you're on. If the name differs, you are probably on a spoofed site.

4. Read Your Statements—Do not toss aside your monthly account statements. Read them thoroughly as soon as they arrive to make sure that all transactions shown are ones that you actually made, and check to see whether all of the transactions that you thought you made appear as well. Be sure that the company has current contact information for you including your mailing address and email address.

5. Spot the Sharks—Visit the website of the Anti-Phishing Working Group at www.antiphishing.org for a list of current phishing attacks and the latest news in the fight to prevent phishing.

What to Do if You Run into Trouble

Always act quickly when you come face to face with a potential fraud, especially if you have lost money or believe your identity has been stolen. If a phishing scam appears in your email box, be sure to tell the company right away. You can also report the scam to the FBI's Internet Fraud Complaint Center at www. IFCCFBI.gov. If the email purports to come from a brokerage firm or mutual fund company, be sure to pass along that tip to the SEC's Enforcement Division by forwarding the email to enforcement@sec.gov.

4

FACTA

The Fair and Accurate Credit Transaction Act of 2003 (FACTA) added new sections to the federal Fair Credit Reporting Act intended to help consumers fight crime of identity theft. Accuracy, privacy, limits on information sharing, and new consumer rights to disclosure are included in FACTA.

Credit Monitoring

Consumer advocates have long encouraged individuals to monitor their credit reports as a way to detect identity theft. The standard advice was to request a copy of your credit report once a year from each of the three national credit bureaus: Experian, TransUnion, and Equifax. Until FACTA, you usually had to pay up to $9.50 to get a copy of your report from each of these credit bureaus.

FACTA also gives you new rights to a free credit report if you are a victim of identity theft. In addition to free credit reports, FACTA gives you the right to one free report annually from a consumer reporting agency that compiles reports on employment, medical records, check writing, insurance, and housing rental history.

Seven states have laws giving their residents a free credit report annually: Colorado, Georgia (two per year), Maine, Maryland, Massachusetts, New Jersey, and Vermont. If you live in one of these states, you can obtain a free report from each bureau annually under federal law and an additional free report under your state's law.

If you are the victim of identity theft, FACTA gives you the right to contact a credit reporting agency to flag your account. To place a fraud alert, you must provide proof of your identity to the credit bureau. The fraud alert is initially effective for 90 days but may be extended at your request for seven years when you provide a police report to the credit bureaus that indicates you are a victim of identity theft.

Active Military Alert

FACTA created a new kind of alert that allows active duty military personnel to place a notation on their credit report as a way to alert potential creditors to possible fraud. While on duty outside the country, military members are particularly vulnerable to identity theft and lack the means to monitor their credit activity. An active duty alert is maintained for at least 12 months.

If a fraud alert or active duty alert is placed on your credit report, any business that is asked to extend credit to you must contact you at a telephone number you provide or take other "reasonable steps" to see that the credit application was not made by an identity thief.

Fraud Alerts

FACTA gives you the right to a free copy of your credit report when you place a fraud alert. With the extended alert (seven years), you are entitled to two free copies of your report during the 12-month period after you place the alert.

New FACTA provisions also allow you to "block" certain items on your credit report that resulted from identity theft. Like the fraud alert, "blocking" was already an option for consumers in some states. With FACTA, Congress has made "blocking" the national standard.

Credit Card Receipts

Credit card receipts that include full account numbers and expiration dates are a gold mine for identity thieves. FACTA requires that credit and debit card receipts may not include more than the last five digits of the card number, nor may the card's expiration date be printed on the cardholder's receipt. However, there are a few exceptions:

- This section does not apply to receipts for which the sole means of recording a credit or debt card number is by handwriting or by an imprint or copy of the card.
- For machines in use before January 1, 2005, the merchant has three years to comply.

- For machines in use after January 1, 2005, the merchant has one year to comply.

Another FACTA section allows consumers who request a copy of their file to also request that the first 5 digits of their Social Security number (or similar identification number) not be included in the file.

For victims of identity theft, obtaining copies of the imposter's account application and transactions is an important step toward regaining financial health. A business that provides credit or products and services to someone who fraudulently uses your identity must give you copies of documents such as applications for credit or transaction records. The business must also provide copies of documents to any federal, state, or local law enforcement agency you specify.

Obtaining Documentation

To obtain account documentation you must supply proof of your identity. The business may also ask you to provide a police report and an identity theft affidavit.

You must also:

- Make your request in writing
- Mail the request to the business
- If the business asks, include relevant information about dates and account numbers

Collection Agencies

A call from a collection agency is often the first sign of trouble for an identity theft victim. Under FACTA, if you are contacted by a collection agency about a debt that resulted from the theft of your identity, the collector must inform the creditor. You are entitled to receive all information about this debt such as applications, account statements, and late notices from the creditor that you would be entitled to see if the debt was actually yours. In addition, FACTA states that once a creditor is notified that the debt is the work of an identity thief, they cannot sell the debt or place it for collection.

Shredding

The practice known as "dumpster diving" provides identity thieves with a treasure trove of personal data. Irresponsible information disposal by businesses has been cited in numerous instances of fraud. Now, under new FACTA provisions, consumer reporting agencies and any business that uses a consumer report must adopt procedures for proper document disposal.

The FTC, the federal banking agencies, and the National Credit Union Administration have published regulations to implement the new FACTA Disposal Rule. The FTC's disposal rule applies to consumer reporting agencies as well as to individuals and any business that uses consumer reports.

The FTC lists the following as among those that must comply with the rule:

- Lenders
- Insurers
- Employers
- Landlords
- Government agencies
- Mortgage brokers
- Automobile dealers
- Attorneys and private investigators
- Debt collectors
- Individuals who obtain a credit report on prospective nannies, contractors, or tenants
- Entities that maintain information in consumer reports as part of their role as service providers to other organizations covered by the rule

Notice of Your Rights

Credit reporting agencies have a new obligation to give identity theft victims a notice of their rights. This includes notice of the right to file a fraud alert, the right to block information in a report that resulted from fraud, and the right to obtain copies of documents used to commit fraud.

Credit Score

It has become increasingly common for lenders to make decisions based upon a "score." Until recently, consumers did not have access to their credit score or information about the factors that made up the score.

Even if you do not have a history of late payments, your score may be lowered if your credit card balance is close to the limit or if you are just starting out with using credit. If you are looking for a car loan or considering refinancing your mortgage, it is a good idea to check your score before you apply for new credit.

FACTA defines a "credit score" as:

"A numerical value or categorization derived from a statistical tool or modeling system used by a person who makes or arranges a loan to predict the likelihood of certain credit behaviors, including default."

The definition does not include a mortgage score. FACTA provides separate requirements for scores generated for home loans and mortgage lenders. In addition, the score consumers are entitled to see under FACTA is an "educational" score intended to inform consumers about how scoring works. This is not the FICO score that lenders are likely to view.

FACTA now requires creditors to give you what might be called an "early warning" notice. This notice could alert you that something is amiss with an account. However, the notice is not a substitute for your own monitoring of credit reports, bank accounts, and credit card statements.

Financial institutions that extend credit must send you a notice before or no later than 30 days after negative information is furnished to a credit bureau. Negative information includes late payments, missed payments, partial payments, or any other form of default on the account.

This is a one-time notice as long as the late payment or other negative information has to do with the same account. After the one-time notice, the financial institution can continue to report negative information about the same account. For example, if you are late on your credit card payment three months straight, you are only entitled to the notice either before or within 30 days after the first late payment is reported.

Medical Information

Under a new FACTA provision, consumer reporting agencies may not report the name, address, and telephone number of any medical creditor unless the information is provided in codes that do not identify the provider of care or the individual's medical condition. Another section of FACTA says a creditor may not obtain or use medical information to make credit decisions. This rule prohibits a creditor from obtaining and using medical information to decide a consumer's credit eligibility. Creditors can still obtain and use financial information if related to medical debts, expenses, and income.

One example is a debt for medical bills. You may owe money to a hospital and perhaps you worked out a plan to pay the debt over time. If you apply for a car loan, the bank can check to see if your payments on the hospital bill are up-to-date. If you are late on your payments, the bank may consider this in deciding whether to give you the loan. The bank cannot, however, ask about your medical condition or the reason for your hospital stay. In other words, the late payments to the hospital cannot carry any more weight than a late payment on a credit card. It is only your history of paying debts that is allowed and your health status should not factor into a creditor's decision about whether to give you a loan.

Under FACTA, your consent to use medical data for employment and credit purposes must be specific and in writing. Further, the consent request must use "clear and conspicuous language" about how the information will be used. FACTA also requires that the medical information requested for employment or credit purposes be "relevant."

Consumer Reports

Consumer reports are generally thought to mean "credit" reports issued by one of the three national credit bureaus: Experian, TransUnion, or Equifax. However, consumer reports may also be issued for purposes other than credit applications. FCRA also covers reports for insurance, employment, check writing, and housing rental history. Such reports are quite common and a number of companies now specialize in providing reports for these specific purposes.

FACTA defines companies that issue non-credit reports as "nationwide specialty consumer reporting agencies" when reports relate to:

- Medical records or payments

- Residential or tenant history

- Check writing history

- Employment history

- Insurance claims

Consumers may request a free report annually from any of the specialty agencies.

Reports about your check writing history are also "specialty" reports and include reports obtained by banks or other financial institutions from ChexSystems. ChexSystems is a consumer reporting agency that collects information from member financial institutions. If, for example, your checking account was closed because of overdrafts, this may appear on a ChexSystems report when you apply to open an account at another bank. Identity theft victims who have had checks stolen may also have a negative ChexSystems report.

Check writing history reports also cover information compiled and reported to member retailers. Check verification systems include information about returned checks or fraud. Check verification works at point of sale. If, for example, you have a check returned, the merchant will probably report this to a verification network. When the same checking account is offered to purchase something from another merchant the check may be rejected. Identity theft or other check fraud may result in a negative entry with a check verification system. Two major check verifications systems are SCAN and TeleCheck.

For bank and merchant verification reports:

- ChexSystems, www.chexsystems.com, (800) 428-9623

- Shared Check Authorization Network (SCAN), (800) 262-7771

- TeleCheck www.telecheck.com, (800) 835-3243

Employee Reports

FACTA sets a new standard for what the law calls "employee misconduct investigations." This is an investigation conducted by a third-party your employer may hire if the employer suspects you of:

- Misconduct relating to your employment

- A violation of federal, state, or local laws or regulations

- A violation of any written policies of the employer
- Noncompliance with the rules of a self-regulatory organization that, for example, oversees the securities and commodity futures industry

This section was adopted to make it clear that employers do not have to get permission to conduct a misconduct investigation. Prior to this, the FTC issued an opinion letter which said the disclosure and consent requirement of FCRA applies even when an employee is suspected of misconduct and the employer hires an outside investigator. Employers objected to this interpretation of the law because they felt that obtaining consent would tip off the employee to an investigation.

Your employer does not have to give you notice or get your permission to conduct a misconduct investigation. Like other inquiries covered by the FCRA, this only applies if the employer hires an outside party to conduct the investigation.

It also means you will not receive a notice of your rights as others who are subject to a standard employment background check normally would. If at the end of the investigation the employer decides to take some action against you, you will receive the "adverse action" notice only after the action has been taken. You will receive only a summary of the investigation report but not the more detailed report that may include sources.

The report may be communicated to:

- The employer or its agent
- Any federal or state officer, agency or department, or any officer, agency or department of a unit of general local government
- Any self-regulatory organization with regulatory authority over the activities of the employer or the employee
- A government agency, in accordance with an existing FCRA section, that allows a consumer reporting agency to disclose personal identifying information to a government agency

You cannot dispute the findings under the FCRA dispute procedure. This is because this new section on workplace misconduct investigations was established by removing this type of investigation from the definition of "consumer report." Thus, the usual protections that apply to a consumer report conducted for employment purposes do not apply to workplace misconduct investigations. If you find yourself in this position you will probably want to seek the advice of an employment law attorney.

Opt-Out Options

FACTA gives consumers a new opportunity to stop an organization's affiliates from sharing customer data for marketing purposes. This opt-out is in addition to the existing opt-out choices.

Existing provisions of the FCRA allow affiliates to share information about your "experience and transactions." This section of the FCRA enables you to stop affiliates from sharing information about your "creditworthiness," also sometimes called "application information." FACTA does not change these procedures, but adds a new opt-out choice to stop information sharing among affiliates when the purpose is for marketing. You now have the ability to prevent the affiliate receiving your information to solicit you for its products and services.

Interest Notification

The amount you pay in interest can vary greatly. If you have a poor credit history, you will usually have to pay a higher rate than people with a good history of repayments. Like many people, you probably receive direct mail or other solicitations quoting exceptionally low interest rates. If you apply for the loan or credit card, though, the interest rate may end up being several points higher than originally quoted.

A new section of FACTA says you must receive a notice if you are offered credit on terms that are "materially" less favorable than others you received from the creditor. In short, this covers the situation where you apply for a loan and, although you get the loan, you have to pay a higher interest rate than others because of something in your credit history. If this happens, you are entitled to a notice plus a free copy of your credit report.

5

Social Security Number Safety

When Social Security Numbers were first issued in 1936, the federal government assured the public that use of the numbers would be limited to Social Security programs. Today, the Social Security Number (SSN) is the most frequently used recordkeeping number in the United States. Social Security Numbers are used for employee files, medical records, health insurance accounts, credit and banking accounts, and many other purposes. In fact, the Social Security Number is now required for dependents over one year of age if the parents claim the child for tax purposes.

Some government agencies, including tax authorities, welfare offices and state Departments of Motor Vehicles, can require your Social Security Number as mandated by federal law. Others may request the social security number in such a manner that you are led to believe you must provide it.

The Privacy Act of 1974 requires all government agencies that request social security numbers to provide a disclosure statement on the form. This statement explains if you are required to provide your Social Security Number or if it is optional, how the social security number will be used, and under what statutory or other authority the number is requested.

The Privacy Act states that you cannot be denied a government benefit or service if you refuse to disclose your social security number unless the disclosure is required by federal law, or the disclosure is to an agency which has been using social security numbers previous to January 1975, the date when the Privacy Act went into effect.

Your employer can use your social security number as an employee identification number. However, the Social Security Administration discourages employers from displaying Social Security Numbers on documents that are viewed by other people such as badges, parking permits, or on lists distributed to employees.

Schools have some interesting laws regarding use of your social security number. Publicly funded schools and those that receive federal funding must comply with the Family Educational Rights and Privacy Act (FERPA) in order to retain their funding. One of FERPA's provisions requires written consent for the release of educational records or personally identifiable information, with some exceptions. Social Security Numbers fall within this provision.

FERPA only applies to state colleges, universities and technical schools that receive federal funding. An argument can be made that if such a school displays students' social security numbers on identification cards or distributes class rosters or grades listings containing social security numbers, it would be a release of personally identifiable information violating FERPA. However, many schools and universities have not interpreted the law this way and continue to use social security numbers as a student identifier. Social Security Numbers may also be obtained by colleges and universities for students who have university jobs or receive federal financial aid.

States cannot use your social security number as your driver license number. The Intelligence Reform and Terrorism Prevention Act of 2004 prohibits states from displaying your social security number on driver licenses or on motor vehicle registrations. This law went into effect on December 17, 2005 and applies to all licenses, registrations, and identification cards issued after that date.

6

Six Computer Safety Tips

Depending on how you use your personal computer, an identity thief may not even need to set foot in your house to steal your personal information.

These tips can help you keep your computer—and the personal information it stores—safe.

1. Virus protection software should be updated regularly and patches for your operating system and other software programs should be installed to protect against intrusions and infections that can lead to the compromise of your computer files or passwords. Your virus protection software should be set to automatically update each week.

2. Do not open files sent to you by strangers, click on hyperlinks, or download programs from people you don't know. You should also be careful about using file sharing programs. Opening a file could expose your system to a computer virus or a program known as "spyware," which could capture your passwords or any other information as you type it into your keyboard.

3. Use a firewall program, especially if you use a high-speed Internet connection like cable, DSL or T-1 where your computer is connected to the Internet 24 hours a day. The firewall program will allow you to stop uninvited access to your computer. Without it, hackers can take over your computer, access the personal information stored on it, or use it to commit other crimes.

4. Use a secure browser which is software that encrypts or scrambles information you send over the Internet. Be sure your browser has the most up-to-date encryption capabilities. When submitting information, look for the "lock" icon on the browser's status bar to be sure your information is secure during transmission.

5. Do not store financial information on your laptop unless absolutely necessary. If you do, use a strong password which is a combination of letters (upper and lower case), and numbers. Do not use an automatic log-in feature that saves your user name and password and always log off when you are finished.

6. Before you dispose of a computer, delete all the personal information it stored. Deleting files using the keyboard or mouse commands may not be enough because the files may stay on the computer's hard drive where they may be retrieved easily. Use a "wipe" utility program to overwrite the entire hard drive.

7

Forty Ways to Prevent Identity Theft

Credit Cards, Debit Cards, and Credit Reports

1. Reduce the number of credit and debit cards you carry in your wallet. Ideally, you should not use debit cards because of the potential for losses to your checking account. Instead, carry just one or two credit cards and your ATM card with you. If you do use debit cards, use the online access to your bank account to monitor account activity frequently and report any amount of fraud to your financial institution immediately. Sometimes, identity thieves will start off with a small amount before stealing a large sum of money from you.

2. When using your credit and debit cards at restaurants and stores, pay close attention to how the magnetic stripe information is swiped by the waiter or clerk. Dishonest employees can use small hand-held devices called skimmers to quickly swipe the card and then later download the account number data onto a personal computer. Also, cut up the hotel keys because the magnetic strip may contain your personal information.

3. Do not use debit cards when shopping online because of the far greater protection with credit cards.

4. Keep a list or copy of all your credit cards, debit cards, bank accounts, investment account numbers, expiration dates and telephone numbers of the customer service and fraud departments in a secure place so you can quickly contact the companies in case your credit cards have been stolen or accounts are being used fraudulently.

5. Never give out your Social Security Number, credit or debit card number or other personal information over the phone, by mail, or on the Internet unless you

have a trusted business relationship with the company and you have initiated the call.

6. Always take credit card receipts with you and never throw them away in a public trash container. When shopping, put receipts in your wallet rather than in the shopping bag.

7. Watch the mail when you are expecting a new or reissued credit card to arrive and contact the issuer if the card does not arrive.

8. Order your credit report at least once a year. Federal law gives you the right to one free credit report each year from the three credit bureaus: Equifax, Experian, and TransUnion. If you are a victim of identity theft, your credit report will show inquiries that were not generated by you as well as credit accounts that you did not open. The earlier you detect fraud, the easier and quicker it will be to clean up your credit files and regain your financial health.

You can stagger your requests to obtain one report every four months to monitor your credit reports on an ongoing basis.

9. Residents in seven states can obtain free annual credit reports under state law in addition to the free reports available under federal law. These states are: Colorado, Maine, Massachusetts, Maryland, New Jersey, Vermont, and Georgia (two free reports per year in Georgia). If you live in one of these states, be sure to order both your free reports under federal law as well as state law each year.

10. Individuals in several states are now able to "freeze" their credit reports. By freezing your credit reports you can prevent credit issuers from accessing your credit files except when you give permission. This effectively prevents thieves from opening up new credit card and loan accounts. In most states, security freezes are available at no charge to identity theft victims and for a relatively small fee for non-victims.

11. Several companies, including the three credit bureaus, offer credit monitoring services for an annual fee ranging from $80–$200 a year which notify you when there is any activity on your credit report.

12. There are many legal and identity theft products available to you both on a group basis and an individual basis. Check with your employer to see if they offer a group legal insurance and an identity theft plan.

Passwords and PINS

13. When creating passwords and PINs (personal identification numbers), do not use the last four digits of your Social Security Number, your mother's maiden name, your birthdate, middle name, pet's name, consecutive numbers or anything else that could easily be discovered by thieves. It's best to create passwords that combine both upper and lower case letters and numbers.

14. Ask your financial institutions to add extra security protection to your account. Most will allow you to use an additional code or password when accessing your account. Do not use your mother's maiden name, Social Security Number, or date of birth. If asked to create a reminder question, do not use one that is easily answered by others.

15. Do not record any of your passwords in your wallet or purse.

16. Shield your hand when using an ATM. "Shoulder surfers" may be nearby with binoculars or video cameras.

Social Security Numbers

17. Protect your Social Security Number and release it only when absolutely necessary.

If a business requests your social security number, ask if it has an alternative number that can be used instead. Speak to a manager or supervisor if your request is not honored. Ask to see the company's written policy on Social Security Numbers and, if necessary, take your business elsewhere. If the social security number is requested by a government agency, look for the Privacy Act notice. This will tell you if your social security number is required, what will be done with it, and what happens if you refuse to provide it.

If possible, do not provide the social security number on job applications. Offer to provide it only when you are interviewed or when a background check is conducted.

19. Do not have your social security number or driver's license number printed on your checks and do not let merchants hand-write the social security number onto your checks.

20. Do not say your social security number out loud when you are in a public place. Whisper or write it down on a piece of paper instead and be sure to retrieve and shred that paper.

21. Examine your Social Security Personal Earnings and Benefits Estimate Statement each year to check for fraud. The Social Security Administration mails this statement to adult-age social security number holders about three months before their birthday.

22. Do not carry your social security card in your wallet except for situations when it is required. If possible, do not carry wallet cards that display your Social Security Number, such as insurance cards, except when needed.

Internet and Computer Safeguards

23. Install a firewall on your computer to prevent hackers from obtaining personal identifying and financial data from your hard drive. This is especially important if you connect to the Internet by DSL or cable modem.

24. Install and update virus protection software to prevent a worm or virus from causing your computer to send out files or other stored information.

25. Password-protect files that contain sensitive personal data such as financial account information. Create passwords that combine 6–8 numbers and letters, upper and lower case. You should also encrypt sensitive files.

26. When shopping online, do business with companies that provide transaction security protection and that have strong privacy and security policies.

27. Before disposing of your computer, remove data by using a strong "wipe" utility program. Do not rely on the "delete" function to remove files containing sensitive information.

28. Never respond to "phishing" email messages. These appear to be from your bank, eBay, or PayPal and instruct you to visit their web site which looks just like the real thing. There, you are told to confirm your account information, provide your Social Security Number, date of birth and other personal information. Legitimate financial companies never email their customers with such requests.

29. Be aware that file-sharing and file-swapping programs expose your computer to illegitimate access by hackers and fraudsters. Install and update strong firewall

and virus protection if you use such programs and make sure you comply with the law. Many file-sharing programs are downloaded by youngsters without the knowledge of their parents.

Reducing Access to Your Personal Data

30. If possible, do not carry other cards in your wallet that contain the Social Security Number (SSN), except on days when you need them.

31. To reduce the amount of personal information that is "out there," take these steps:

- Remove your name from the marketing lists of the three credit reporting bureaus—Equifax, Experian, and TransUnion. Call 888-5OPTOUT or go online to www.optoutprescreen.com. This will limit the number of pre-approved offers of credit that you receive. These, when tossed into the garbage without being shredded, are a potential target of identity thieves who use them to order credit cards in your name.

- Sign up for the Federal Trade Commission's National Do Not Call Registry. Your name is added to name deletion lists used by nationwide marketers. You may also need to register for your state's "do not call" list, if it has one.

  - National Do Not Call Registry, www.donotcall.gov, (888) 382-1222

  - FTC's Do Not Call FAQ, www.ftc.gov/bcp/conline/pubs/alerts/dncalrt.htm

- Sign up for the Direct Marketing Association's Mail Preference Service at www.dmaconsumers.org/cgi/offmailinglist.

- Have your name and address removed from the phone book and reverse directories.

- Opt-out of the sale or sharing of your financial information when given the opportunity.

32. Install a locked mailbox at your residence to deter mail theft, or use a post office box or a commercial mailbox service. When you are away from home for an extended time, have your mail held at the Post Office or ask a trusted neighbor to pick it up.

33. When ordering new checks, pick them up at the bank. Do not have them mailed to your home. If you have a post office box, use that address on your checks rather than your home address so thieves will not know where you live.

34. When you pay bills, do not leave the envelopes containing your checks at your mailbox for the postal carrier to pick up or in open boxes at the receptionist's desk in your workplace. If stolen, your checks can be altered and then cashed by the imposter. It is best to mail bills and other sensitive items at the drop boxes inside the post office rather than neighborhood drop boxes.

Responsible Information Handling

35. Each month carefully review your credit card, bank and phone statements, including cellular phone bills, for unauthorized use.

36. Convert as much bill-paying as you can to automatic deductions from your checking account and/or credit account and consider using the Internet for banking and paying bills. With fewer account statements and bills mailed to your home, you will reduce the risk of mail theft and identity theft.

37. Do not toss pre-approved credit offers in your trash or recycling bin without first tearing them into very small pieces or shredding them with a cross-cut shredder. They can be used by "dumpster divers" to order credit cards in your name and mail them to their address. You should also do the same with other sensitive information like credit card receipts, phone bills, bank account statements, and investment account reports.

38. Use a gel pen for writing checks. Gel ink contains tiny particles of color that are trapped in the paper making check washing more difficult.

39. Store canceled checks in a safe place. In the wrong hands, they could reveal a lot of information about you including your account number, phone number and driver license number. If you rent a storage locker, take extra precautions when storing cancelled checks, tax return information, and other sensitive financial information. Storage lockers are popular targets for identity thieves.

40. Store personal information securely in your home, especially if you have roommates, employ outside help, or have service work done in your home. Use a locking file cabinet or safe.

8

20 Things to Do if You Are a Victim of Identity Theft

1. Immediately report the situation to the fraud department of the three credit reporting companies—Experian, Equifax, and TransUnion. When you notify one bureau that you are at risk of being a victim of identity theft, it will notify the other two for you. Placing the fraud alert means that your file will be flagged and that creditors are required to call you before extending credit.

Under new provisions of the Fair Credit Reporting Act (FACRA) you can place an initial fraud alert for 90 days and the credit bureaus will mail you a notice of your rights as an identity theft victim. Once you receive them, contact each of the three bureaus immediately to request two things:

- A free copy of your credit report
- An extension of the fraud alert to seven years

You must have evidence of attempts to open fraudulent accounts and an identity theft report (police report) to establish the seven-year alert and you may cancel the fraud alerts at any time.

In all communications with the credit bureaus you will want to refer to the unique number assigned to your credit report and use certified, return receipt mail. Be sure to save all credit reports as part of your fraud documentation file.

Once you have received your three credit reports, examine each one carefully. Report fraudulent accounts and erroneous information in writing to both the credit bureaus and the credit issuers following the instructions provided with the credit reports.

Once you notify the credit bureaus about the fraudulent accounts, the bureau is required to block that information from future reports. The bureau must also notify the credit grantor of the fraudulent account. Ask the credit bureaus for the names and phone numbers of credit grantors with whom fraudulent accounts have been opened if this information is not included on the credit report.

Instruct the credit bureaus in writing to remove inquiries that have been generated due to the fraudulent access. You may also ask the credit bureaus to notify those who have received your credit report in the last six months to alert them to the disputed and erroneous information.

Monitor your credit reports and be aware that these measures may not entirely prevent new fraudulent accounts from being opened by the imposter. Credit issuers do not always pay attention to fraud alerts even though the law now requires it.

FACTA enables you to receive a free credit report per year from each of the three credit bureaus. This is over and above the free reports you can order when you place fraud alerts on your three credit reports. Once you have received your free credit reports as a part of the fraud-alert process, follow up in a few months by taking advantage of your free FACTA copy.

2. Report the crime to your local police or sheriff's department immediately. You also need to report it to the police department where the crime occurred if it is somewhere other than where you live. Make sure the police report lists the fraudulent accounts and get a copy of the report which is called an "Identity Theft Report" under FCRA. Keep the phone number of your investigator handy and give it to creditors and others who require verification of your case. Credit card companies and banks may require you to show the report in order to verify the crime.

Federal Trade Commission (FTC) regulations define an "Identity Theft Report" to include a report made to a local, state, or federal law enforcement agency. If your local police department refuses to file a report and your situation involves fraudulent use of the U.S. mail, you can obtain an identity theft report from the U.S. Postal Inspector. If your case involves fraudulent use of a driver's license in your name, you can obtain a report from your state's Department of Motor Vehicles.

3. Report the crime to the FTC and include your police report number. Although the FTC does not itself investigate identity theft cases, they share information with investigators nationwide who are fighting identity theft.

4. If your credit report shows that the imposter has opened new accounts in your name, contact those creditors immediately by telephone and in writing.

Creditors will most likely ask you to fill out fraud affidavits. Ask the credit grantors in writing to furnish you and your investigating law enforcement agency with copies of the documentation such as the fraudulent application and transaction records.

A victim of identity theft must provide a copy of the FTC affidavit or another affidavit acceptable to the business, plus government-issued identification, and a copy of an "Identity Theft Report" (police report) in order to obtain the documents created by the imposter. The business must provide copies of these records to the victim within 30 days of the victim's request at no charge.

When you have resolved the fraudulent account with the creditor, ask for a letter stating that the company has closed the disputed account and has discharged the debts. Be sure to keep this letter in your files because you may need it if the account reappears on your credit report.

5. If your existing credit or debit accounts have been used fraudulently, report it in writing immediately to the credit card company.

Request replacement cards with new account numbers. In addition to calling the credit card company regarding the fraud, you will need to follow up in writing and will likely be asked to provide a fraud affidavit or a dispute form. Send the letter to the address given for "billing inquiries," not the address for sending payments. Carefully monitor your mail and bills for evidence of new fraudulent activity. You should also add secure passwords to all accounts which should not be your mother's maiden name or any word that is easily guessed.

6. If debt collectors try to get you to pay the unpaid bills on fraudulent accounts, ask for the name of the collection company, the name of the person contacting you, their phone number, and address. Tell the collector that you are a victim of fraud and are not responsible for the account. Ask for the name and contact information for the referring credit issuer, the amount of the debt, account number, and dates of the charges. Ask if they need you to complete their fraud affida-

vit form or whether you can use the FTC affidavit. Follow up by writing to the debt collector explaining your situation. Ask that they confirm in writing that you do not owe the debt and that the account has been closed.

Under new provisions in FCRA, a debt collector must notify the creditor that the debt may be a result of identity theft. FCRA also prohibits the sale or transfer of a debt caused by identity theft.

7. If you have had checks stolen or bank accounts set up fraudulently, ask your bank to report it to ChexSystems, a consumer reporting agency that compiles reports on checking accounts. Also, place a security alert on your file.

Your bank should be able to provide you with a fraud affidavit. Put "stop payments" on any outstanding checks that you are unsure about. Close your checking account and other affected accounts and obtain new account numbers.

8. If your ATM or debit card has been stolen or compromised, report it immediately. Contact your bank and fill out a fraud affidavit. Get a new card, account number, and password. Do not use your old password and closely monitor your account statements. You may be liable if the fraud is not reported quickly. Be sure to read the debit card contract for information about liability because some cards are better protected in cases of fraud than others.

ATM and debit card transactions are subject to the Electronic Fund Transfer Act. Even if you are a victim of identity theft, your liability for charges can increase the longer the crime goes unreported.

9. You do not have the same protections against loss with brokerage accounts as you do with credit and debit card or bank accounts. The Securities Investor Protection Corporation (SIPC) restores customer funds only when a brokerage firm fails. If an identity thief or other fraudster targets your brokerage account, refer to your account agreement for information on what to do. Immediately report the incident to the brokerage company and notify the Securities and Exchange Commission. Also notify the National Association of Securities Dealers.

10. Notify the local Postal Inspector if you suspect an unauthorized change of your address with the post office or if the U.S mail has been used to commit fraud. Find out where fraudulent credit cards were sent and notify the local Postmaster to forward all mail in your name to your own address.

11. Although the Social Security Administration (SSA) does not in most cases provide assistance to identity theft victims, be sure to contact the SSA Inspector General to report Social Security benefit fraud, employment fraud, or welfare fraud.

As a last resort, you might try to change your number, although it is not recommended except for very serious cases. The SSA will only change the number if you fit their fraud victim criteria.

If your social security number has been stolen or lost, order a replacement. Call the SSA at (800) 772-1213, or by visiting your local SSA office. You will need to provide the required documentation such as birth certificate and government ID at your local SSA office to get a replacement card.

12. Whether you have a passport or not, write to the passport office to alert them to anyone ordering a passport fraudulently.

- U.S. Department of State, Passport Services, Consular Lost/Stolen Passport Section, 1111 19th Street, NW, Suite 500, Washington, DC 20036.
- Website: www.travel.state.gov/passport/lost/lost_849.html

13. Identity thieves often establish fraudulent cell phone accounts with monthly bills going unpaid. The imposter might also open local and long distance telephone accounts. If the imposter has obtained phone accounts in your name, contact the phone company for information on how to report the situation.

If your calling card has been stolen or there are fraudulent charges, cancel it and open a new account. For your own phone accounts, add a password that must be used any time your local, cell phone, and long distance accounts are changed.

14. If an identity thief has obtained a student loan in your name, report it in writing to the school that opened the loan and request that the account be closed. Also report it to the U.S. Department of Education:

Office of Inspector General, U.S. Department of Education, 400 Maryland Avenue, SW, Washington, DC 20202-1510, (800) MISUSED (800-647-8733)

Web: www.ed.gov/about/offices/list/oig/hotline.html?src=rt

15. You may also need to change your driver license number if someone is using yours as an ID on bad checks or for other types of fraud. Call the Department of

Motor Vehicles (DMV) to see if another license was issued in your name. Put a fraud alert on your license if your state's DMV provides a fraud alert process and go to your local DMV to request a new number.

16. Sometimes victims of identity theft are wrongfully accused of crimes that were committed by the imposter. If you are wrongfully arrested or prosecuted for criminal charges, contact the police department and the court in the jurisdiction of the arrest. Also contact your state's Department of Justice and the FBI to ask how to clear your name. If a civil judgment is entered in your name for your imposter's actions, contact the court where the judgment was entered and report that you are a victim of identity theft.

17. You may want to consult an attorney to determine legal action to take against creditors, credit bureaus, and/or debt collectors if they are not cooperative in removing fraudulent entries from your credit report or if negligence is a factor. Call your local Bar Association, a Legal Aid office in your area, or the National Association of Consumer Advocates to find an attorney who specializes in consumer law, the Fair Credit Reporting Act, and the Fair Credit Billing Act.

If you are a senior citizen or take care of a dependent adult, be sure to contact an elder law service or the nearest Aging and Independent Services program. Many district attorneys have an elder abuse unit with expertise in financial crimes against seniors.

18. In dealing with the authorities and financial companies, keep a log of all conversations including dates, names, and phone numbers. Note the time you spent and any expenses incurred in case you are able to seek restitution in a later judgment or conviction against the thief. You may also be able to obtain tax deductions for theft-related expenses. Confirm all conversations in writing and send correspondence using certified mail with return receipt requested.

19. Do not pay any bill or portion of a bill that is a result of fraud and do not cover any checks that were written or cashed fraudulently. Your credit rating should not be permanently affected and no legal action should be taken against you. If any merchant, financial company or collection agency suggests otherwise, restate your willingness to cooperate, but don't allow yourself to be coerced into paying fraudulent bills.

20. If you are in the military, place an active duty alert on your credit report. When you are away from your usual duty station you can place an active duty

alert on your three credit reports as an extra protection against identity theft. The alert remains on your credit reports for 12 months.

9

Twelve Online Shopping Tips

With just a click of the mouse you can buy nearly any product online. The world of electronic commerce enables you to shop at thousands of online stores and pay for your purchases without leaving the comfort of your home.

You expect merchants to not only make their products available on the web, but also to make payments a simple and secure process. However, the same things can go wrong shopping in cyberspace as in the real world. Sometimes it is simply a case of a computer glitch or poor customer service. Other times, shoppers are cheated by clever scam artists.

The top security concerns of America's online shoppers include:

- Email addresses being sold to third parties

- Fears about personal or financial information being stolen

- Email scans known as "phishing" or "spoofing" in which you receive messages from dishonest sources disguised as messages from trusted retailers or financial institutions

1. Shop at Secure Web Sites

A secure website uses encryption technology to transfer information from your computer to the online merchant's computer. Encryption scrambles the information you send, such as your credit card number, in order to prevent computer hackers from obtaining it en route. The only people who can unscramble the code are those with legitimate access privileges.

You can tell when you are dealing with a secure web site in several ways.

- First, if you look at the top of your screen where the web site address is displayed, you should see https://. The "s" that is displayed after "http" indicates that web site is secure. Often, you do not see the "s" until you actually move to the order page on the web site.

- Another way to determine if a web site is secure is to look for a closed padlock displayed at the bottom of your screen. If that lock is open, you should assume it is not a secure site.

- The third symbol that indicates you are on a secure site is an unbroken key.

2. Research the Web Site before You Order

If the company is unfamiliar to you, do your homework before buying their products. If you decide to buy something from an unknown company, start out with an inexpensive order to learn if the company is trustworthy.

Reliable companies should advertise their physical business address and at least one phone number. Call the phone number and ask questions to determine if the business is legitimate. Ask how the merchant handles returned merchandise and complaints and find out if it offers full refunds or only store credits.

You can also research a company in the Internet yellow pages, through the Better Business Bureau, or a government consumer protection agency like the district attorney's office or the Attorney General. Remember, most anyone can create a good looking web site.

3. Read the Web Site's Privacy and Security Policies

Every reputable e-commerce web site offers information about how it processes your order and it is usually listed in the section entitled "Privacy Policy." You can find out if the merchant intends to share your information with a third party or affiliate company.

Look for online merchants who are members of a seal-of-approval program that sets voluntary guidelines for privacy-related practices, such as TRUSTe (www.truste.org), Verisign (www.verisign.com), or BBBonline (www.bbbon-line.org).

4. What's Safest: Credit Cards, Debit Cards, Cash, or Checks?

The safest way to shop on the Internet is with a credit card. In the event something goes wrong, you are protected under the federal Fair Credit Billing Act.

You have the right to dispute charges on your credit card and you can withhold payments during a creditor investigation. When your credit is used without authorization, you are only responsible for the first $50 in charges and you are rarely asked to pay this charge. It is best to have one credit card that you use only for online payments to make it easier to detect wrongful credit charges.

Make sure your credit card is a true credit card and not a debit card, a check card, or an ATM card. As with checks, a debit card exposes your bank account to thieves and your checking account could be wiped out in minutes. Further, debit and ATM cards are not protected by federal law to the extent that credit cards are.

5. Never, Never Give Out Your Social Security Number

Providing your Social Security Number is not a requirement for placing an order at an e-commerce web site and there is absolutely no need for the merchant to ask for it.

6. Disclose Only the Bare Facts When You Order

When placing an order, there is certain information that you must provide to the web merchant such as your name and address. Often, though, a merchant will try to obtain more information about you. This information is used to target you for marketing purposes and can lead to spam, direct mail, and telephone solicitations.

7. Keep Your Password Private

Most reputable e-commerce web sites require you to log in before placing or viewing an order and you are usually required to provide a username and a password. When selecting a password, do not use commonly known information such as your birthdate, mother's maiden name, or numbers from your driver's license or Social Security Number, and do not reuse the same password for other sites. The best passwords have at least eight characters and include numbers and letters.

8. Check the Web Site Address

Above the web site at the top of your screen is a rectangular window that contains the web site address. By checking that address, you can make sure that you are dealing with the correct company.

Identity thieves send massive numbers of emails to Internet users that ask them to update the account information for their banks, credit cards, online payment service, or popular shopping sites. The email may state that your account information has expired, been compromised or lost, and that you need to immediately resend it to the company.

Some emails sent as part of such phishing expeditions often contain links to official looking web pages and other times the emails ask the consumer to download and submit an electronic form. As many as five percent of email recipients respond to phishing becoming victims of financial loss, identity theft, and other crimes.

Legitimate businesses don't ask for sensitive information via email and you should not respond to any request for financial information that comes to you in an email.

9. Always Print Copies of Your Orders

After placing an order online you should receive a confirmation page that reviews your entire order. It should include the costs of the order, your customer information, product information, and the confirmation number.

You should print out at least one copy of the web page describing the items you ordered as well as the page showing the company name, postal address, phone number, and legal terms including their return policy. Often, you will also receive a confirmation message that is e-mailed to you by the merchant. Be sure to save or print this message as well as any other e-mail correspondence with the company.

10. Shop with Companies Located in the United States

When you shop within the U.S., you are protected by state and federal consumer laws. You might not get the same protection if you place an order with a company located in another country.

11. Use Your Shopper's Intuition

Look at the site with a critical eye and heed the old adage—"If it looks too good to be true, it probably is."

- Are there extraordinary claims that you question?

- Do the company's prices seem unusually low?

- Does it look like the merchant is an amateur?

- Are there spelling or grammar errors?

- Does the company's phone go unanswered?

If any of these questions trigger a warning bell, you will be wise to find another online merchant.

12. Consider Using Single-Use Card Numbers

Consumers using some brands of credit cards can get "virtual credit cards," or single-use card numbers, that can be used at an online store. The randomly generated substitute 16-digit number can also be used to buy goods and services over the phone and through the mail, but can't be used for in-store purchases that require a traditional plastic card.

With this service, you never need to give out your real credit card number online. Among the card companies offering it are Citibank and the Discover card.

10

Current State Credit Freeze Laws

✦

(as of 2008)

California

- Effective January 1, 2003
- Applies to all consumers
- No fee for victims to place the freeze and others pay up to $10 per freeze
- Fee to lift freeze is $10 for a temporary lifting and $12 for a temporary lift for one creditor

Colorado

- Effective July 1, 2006
- Applies to all consumers
- No fee for the first freeze and $10 to place a second freeze, $10 to lift a freeze, and $12 for a temporary lift for one creditor

Connecticut

- Effective January 1, 2006
- Applies to all consumers
- $10 to place, lift, or lift temporarily and $12 to lift for one creditor

Delaware

- Effective September 28, 2006

- Applies to all consumers
- $20 to place a freeze, free to temporarily lift for a period of time or for a specific creditor and to remove

District of Columbia

- Effective July 1, 2007

- Applies to all consumers

- $10 for an initial placement and free for victims of identity theft with no fees to remove permanently or temporarily

Florida

- Effective July 1, 2006
- Applies to all consumers
- No fees for victims of identity theft (with investigative report) and seniors age 65 or older
- For all others, $10 to place, temporarily lift, or remove

Hawaii

- Effective January 1, 2007
- Victims of identity theft only with a police, investigative report, or complaint filed with a law enforcement agency
- No fees

Illinois

- Effective January 1, 2007
- Applies to all consumers
- No fee for victims of identity theft with a police report and seniors age 65 or older to place, remove or temporarily remove

Kansas

- Effective January 1, 2007

- Victims of identity theft only with a police, investigative report or a complaint filed with a law enforcement agency
- No fees

Kentucky

- Effective July 11, 2006
- Applies to all consumers
- No fees for identity theft victims who provide a police report
- Others pay $10 to place, remove, temporarily suspend or have a PIN reissued
- Expires seven years from date of placement or upon the consumer's request, if earlier

Louisiana

- Effective July 1, 2005
- Applies to all consumers
- $10 to place and $8 to lift
- No fees for identity theft victims or seniors age 62 or older

Maine

- Effective February 1, 2006
- Applies to all consumers
- No fees for identity theft victims who provide a police report
- $10 to place, remove, temporarily suspend, or have a PIN reissued
- $12 to lift the freeze for a specific creditor

Minnesota

- Effective August 1, 2006
- Applies to all consumers
- No fees for identity theft victims who provide a police report

- $5 to place, remove, temporarily suspend, lift for a specific creditor, or have the PIN reissued

Nevada

- Effective October 1, 2005
- Applies to all consumers
- No fees for identity theft victims who provide a police report
- $15 to place, $18 to lift, $20 to lift for one creditor

New Hampshire

- Effective January 1, 2007
- Applies to all consumers
- No fees for identity theft victims who provide a police report, investigative report, or complaint to a law enforcement agency
- $10 to place, temporarily lift, or remove

New Jersey

- Effective January 1, 2006
- Applies to all consumers
- No fees for initial freeze
- $5 to remove, temporarily lift, or have the PIN reissued

New York

- Effective November 1, 2006
- Applies to all consumers
- Free to place first time for everyone.
- $5 fee after the first time or to lift or temporarily remove
- No fees for identity theft victims

North Carolina

- Effective December 1, 2005

- No fees for identity theft victims who provide a police report, investigative report, or complaint to a law enforcement agency
- $10 to place, remove, or temporarily suspend

Oklahoma

- Effective January 1, 2007
- Applies to all consumers
- No fees for identity theft victims with investigative report and seniors age 65 and older

Pennsylvania

- Effective January 1, 2007
- Applies to all consumers
- No fees for identity theft victims or seniors age 65 or older
- $10 to place freeze
- Freeze lasts seven years

Rhode Island

- Effective January 1, 2007
- Applies to all consumers
- No fees for Identity Theft victims or seniors age 65 or older

South Dakota

- Effective July 1, 2006
- Applies to identity theft victims with a police report
- No fees
- Only freezes credit report
- Lasts seven years or earlier upon consumers request

Texas

- Effective September 1, 2003

- Applies to identity theft victims with a police report
- $8 placement fee

Utah

- Effective September 1, 2008
- Applies to all consumers
- Reasonable fees
- Consumers can temporarily lift or "thaw" freeze within 15 minutes of an electronic request

Vermont

- Effective July 1, 2006
- Applies to all consumers
- No fees for identity theft victims
- $10 to place, $5 to remove or temporarily lift

Washington

- Effective July 24, 2005
- Applies to identity theft victims, including persons who receive a notice of a security breach of computerized personal information
- No fees

Wisconsin

- Effective July 1, 2007
- Applies to all consumers
- No cost to victims of identity theft
- $10 fee for all others

Wyoming

- Effective July 1, 2007
- Requires electronic and telephone methods to lift

- Imposes a 15 minute lift timeframe beginning September 1, 2008
- Fee of $10
- No cost for identity theft victims

11

Sample Identity Theft Letters

Date

Your Name
Mailing Address
City, State, Zip

Re: Disputing Inaccuracies on My Credit Report

Name of Credit Reporting Bureau
Mailing Address
City, State, Zip

Dear Sir or Madam:

I am writing for two reasons:

1. To dispute certain information in my credit file; and

2. To have you investigate/re-investigate and remove inaccurate information from my Credit Report and prevent its re-insertion. The items I dispute are circled on the attached copy of the credit report and further identified by *(identify the items by name of source, such as creditor or tax court, etc. and identify type of item, such as credit account, judgment, etc.)* This item is *(inaccurate or incomplete)* because *(describe what is inaccurate or incomplete and why)*. I am requesting that the item be deleted *(or whatever specific change you are requesting)* to correct the information.*(If you are enclosing documents such as copies of cancelled checks, payment records, court documents, send copies only, you should always retain the originals and use the following sentence.)*

Enclosed are copies of the following documents supporting my position:

Please reinvestigate these matters and correct the disputed items within the time frame required by the Fair Credit Reporting Act (FCRA) and inform me in writing of the outcome. Thank you for your time and consideration in this matter.

Sincerely,

Your Name
Mailing Address
City, State, Zip

Date

Name of Collection Agency
Mailing Address

Re: Dispute of Collection Action: Case # _____

(If the collection agency has sent written notice, your case number is likely in the letter. If you have not received a written notice from the collection agency, tailor this line accordingly. For example, show the date you were contacted by the collection agency and/or identify the creditor by name if you can.)

To *(person whose name appears on agency's notice to you):*

On *(date)* I was contacted by *(name of person who called you)* of your agency, who informed me that *(name of collection agency)* is attempting to collect *(amount of claimed debt)*. This individual is collecting on behalf of *(name of creditor)*.

OR—This individual would not tell me for whom you are supposed to be collecting.

This is to inform you that I dispute the debt because *(insert reason for dispute and copies of any correspondence that proves your point)*. I am hereby requesting that you confirm the fact that I owe this debt as required by any applicable state and federal laws. Please contact the creditor to obtain verification.

In addition, under the provisions of state and federal Fair Debt Collection Practices Act (FDCPA), Fair Credit Reporting Act (FCRA), and related consumer statutes, I am hereby instructing you that you are to cease collection of the debt while efforts are made to obtain verification. Until you resolve this error with the creditor, you should neither contact me nor anyone else except the creditor about this collection.

Furthermore, any reporting of this matter to a credit reporting agency is premature. Until you have investigated my dispute, you should not relay negative information to a credit reporting agency. If negative information has already been reported, you will need to notify the agency to remove said report until the investigative process is over so that my credit report remains accurate, or at the very least, my credit report should be updated to reflect my dispute.

Your next contact with me should be either notice that the creditor has failed to provide verification of the debt and that the matter has been closed or that you believe that this debt is valid and are providing proof of my responsibility. If the former, please confirm that I am not being held responsible for the debt in writing and also that if the account has already been noted on my credit report, that you will contact the bureau in question to have the account removed. If the latter, I expect that you will provide me with an explanation as to why you have decided not to remove this account from collections and a copy of all documents relevant to the debt such as the application, bills, records of communications and payments, and any other data that indicates my responsibility.

I am instructing you not to contact any third parties such as my employer, neighbors, friends or family members. In addition, you may not contact me by phone at work or at my home about this collection activity. All future correspondence should be sent to me in writing.

I look forward to your acknowledgement that you have received this notice by (*date that is two weeks from date of letter*).

Sincerely,

Your Name
Mailing Address
City, State, Zip

Date

Name of Collection Agency
Mailing Address
City, State, Zip

Re: Notice to Cease Contact: Case # _____

(If the collection agency has sent written notice, your case number is likely in the letter. If you have not received a written notice from the collection agency, tailor this line accordingly. For example, show the date you were contacted by the collection agency.)

To *(person whose name appears on agency's notice to you):*

On *(date)* I was contacted by *(name of person who called you)* of your agency, who informed me that *(name of collection agency)* is attempting to collect *(amount of claimed debt).*

This is to give you notice to cease all contact with me or anyone else except the creditor about this claimed debt. If you must contact me, please do so in writing and not by telephone.

I look forward to your acknowledgement that you have received this notice by *(date that is two weeks from date of letter).*

Sincerely,

Your Name
Mailing Address
Your City, State, Zip

Date

Name of Collection Agency
Mailing Address
City, State, Zip

Re: Identity Theft Victim Notice to Cease Contact: Case #_____

(If the collection agency has sent written notice, your case number is likely in the letter. If you have not received a written notice from the collection agency, tailor this line accordingly. For example, show the date you were contacted by the collection agency.)

To *(person whose name appears on agency's notice to you)*:

On *(date)* I was contacted by *(name of person who called you)* of your agency, who informed me that *(name of collection agency)* is attempting to collect *(amount of claimed debt)*.

I am a victim of identity theft. The debt about which your agency contacted me is the result of fraud by someone who used my personal information without my knowledge or consent. I have enclosed a copy of the police report I filed when I learned of the crime. *(Instead of the police report, the Federal Trade Commission identity theft affidavit can be provided.)* Please provide me with any forms such as a fraud affidavit that your company will require me to fill out to have this account properly investigated as fraud if the enclosed FTC Fraud Affidavit is not sufficient.

I have enclosed the following documents to prove my claim of fraud:

(List copies of any documents you enclose with the letter that prove your claim of identity theft. Such documents could be a copy of a police report, copy of your Federal Trade Commission's Fraud Affidavit, or correspondence between you and a credit bureau, a merchant, or a bank. Lease agreements and utility bills often help prove you were living somewhere other than where the account was established.)

This is to give you notice to cease all contact with me or anyone else about this claimed debt except the creditor or consumer reporting agency as necessary to clear my name. I understand that under state and federal law, you may only contact me one more time in order to confirm your receipt of this request.

In addition, the Fair Debt Collection Practices Act gives me the right to a copy of applications or other documents your agency has obtained as proof of the debt. Please forward copies of any such documents you now have or later obtain to me at the above address.

I look forward to your acknowledgement that you have received this notice by *(date that is two weeks from date of letter)*.

Sincerely,

Date

Your Name
Mailing Address
City, State, Zip

Name of Collection Agency
Mailing Address
City, State, Zip

Re: Notice to Stop Third-Party Contacts: Case # _____

(If the collection agency has sent written notice, your case number is likely in the letter. If you have not received a written notice from the collection agency, tailor this line accordingly. For example, show the date you were contacted by the collection agency.)

To *(person whose name appears on agency's notice to you):*

On *(date)* I was contacted by *(name of person who called you)* of your agency, who informed me that *(name of collection agency)* is attempting to collect *(amount of claimed debt).*

(Summarize any contacts the collection agency has had with your employer, family, friends, neighbors, or any other third party.)

This is to inform you that my employer does not permit me to be contacted at my place of employment and any attempt to contact me there could cause me harm or disadvantage. Any disregard of this instruction not to contact me, my friends, relatives or anyone at my employment will result in my seeking legal advice on the full extent of my remedies under state, federal, and common law.

Furthermore, your having contacted me at my address or on my phone number confirms that you have full knowledge of both pieces of information, rendering any contacts with any third parties a violation of my rights as an individual and a consumer under state and federal law.

Please advise me immediately of any contacts to third parties already made by your agency or by your client so that I can attempt to control or undo any damage that may result and take every possible step to make sure that no further attempts at such contacts are made. Please conduct all future correspondence to me directly and in writing.

(Make sure you save all envelopes for their postmark and note on the back of each envelope or in your journal the date each letter is received. This is important because some debt collectors will attempt to back-date correspondence to you, and your post-mark/note will be the only way to prove the falsity of any such tricks.)

I look forward to your acknowledgement that you have received this notice by *(date that is two weeks from date of letter).*

Sincerely,

Date

Your Name
Mailing Address
City, State, Zip

Re: Complaint Against *(Name of Collection Agency),*

Case # _____

Name of Government Agency
City, State, Zip

To *(name of agency official, such as State Attorney General):*

I am writing to complain about the above-named collection agency. This collection agency engaged in the following unfair and abusive collection practices specifically prohibited by the Fair Debt Collection Practices Act, 15 USC §1692.

(Summarize the prohibited practices, the results of said practice and any indications that the violation may have been deliberate. Make special note of any comment by the collector about how long it takes for instructions to be placed in their system. Failure to meet required standards may subject them to additional penalties and loss of defenses to any future claim by you. Some examples follow.)

On *(date, name of collection agency)* contacted me at my place of employment after having been notified in writing that my employer prohibits such contacts.

On *(date, name of collection agency)* called me at _____.

On *(date)* the *(name of collection agency employee)* used obscene and abusive language. *(Add appropriate details here.)*

On *(date)* I received the enclosed documents from *(name of collection agency)* which appeared to be court documents imposing a judgment against me, but were not.

On *(date, name of collection agency employee)* contacted my neighbor, and without being asked, revealed the name of the collection agency and discussed the details of the debt the agency claims I owe.

I request that your agency investigate the practices of *(name of collection agency)* and take appropriate enforcement action to stop these unfair and abusive practices. Thank you.

Sincerely,

Date

Your Name
Mailing Address
Your City, State, Zip

Re: Notice to Cease Contact Regarding Debt for _____

Name of Collection Agency
Mailing Address
City, State, Zip

I am notifying you in writing that your agency has contacted me regarding a debt for *(name of person who collector is contacting you about)*. No one by that name lives at my address or phone number.

Therefore, I am requesting that you cease all communication to my phone number regarding this person's debt. If you persist in believing that [name of person] is somehow connected with my address and/or phone number, please provide proof of your claim.

You should direct all future correspondence in writing as outlined in the Fair Debt Collection Practices Act (FDCPA) and to cease all communication with me by telephone.

Lastly, I would like to receive confirmation in writing that you have received this letter and will no longer be contacting me about this other person's debt, or I will be forced to seek further legal action.

I look forward to your acknowledgement that you have received this notice by *(date that is two weeks from date of letter)*.

Sincerely,

Date

Your Name
Mailing Address
Your City, State, Zip

RE: Opt-Out Instructions for Account #_____

Dear *(name if given in the privacy notice):*

Following are my instructions with regard to your information sharing and sales policies:

1. You do not have my permission to share my personally identifiable information with nonaffiliated third party companies or individuals. I am asserting my rights under the Financial Services Modernization Act (the Gramm-Leach-Bliley Act) to opt-out of any sharing or sales of my information by your company.

2. You do not have my permission to share information about my creditworthiness with any affiliate of your company. I am asserting my rights under the Fair Credit Reporting Act to opt-out of any sharing of this information by your company.

3. *(Optional)* I do not wish to receive marketing offers from your company or its affiliates. Please delete my name from all marketing lists and databases.

(Optional) Your company's privacy notice states you may otherwise use my information as "permitted by law." I wish to limit other uses of my personal information by your company and its affiliates. In particular:

* You do not have my permission to disclose any information about me, including transaction and experience information, to your affiliates.

* You do not have my permission to disclose any information about me in connection with direct marketing agreements between your company and another company.

Thank you for respecting my privacy and honoring my choices regarding my customer information.

Please acknowledge your intention to comply with my request for privacy of my personal financial and other information.

Sincerely,

Date

Your Name
Mailing Address
City, State, Zip

Re: Disputing Inaccuracies on My Credit Report

Name of Credit Reporting Bureau
Mailing Address
City, State, Zip

Dear Sir or Madam:

I am writing for two reasons:

1. To dispute certain information in my credit file; and

2. To have you investigate/re-investigate and remove inaccurate information from my Credit Report and prevent its re-insertion. The items I dispute are encircled on the attached copy of the credit report and further identified by *(identify the items by name of source, such as creditor or tax court, etc. and identify type of item, such as credit account, judgment, etc.)*This item is *(inaccurate or incomplete)* because *(describe what is inaccurate or incomplete and why)*. I am requesting that the item be deleted (or whatever specific change you are requesting) to correct the information.

Enclosed are copies of the following documents supporting my position:

Please reinvestigate this matter and correct the disputed items within the time frame required by the Fair Credit Reporting Act (FCRA) and inform me in writing of the outcome. Thank you for your time and consideration in this matter.

Your Name
Mailing Address
Your City, State, Zip

Date

Name of Collection Agency
Mailing Address
City, State, Zip

Re: Identity Theft Victim Notice to Cease Contact: Case #_____

(If the collection agency has sent written notice, your case number is likely in the letter. If you have not received a written notice from the collection agency, tailor this line accordingly. For example, show the date you were contacted by the collection agency.)

To *(person whose name appears on agency's notice to you):*

On *(date)* I was contacted by *(name of person who called you)* of your agency, who informed me that *(name of collection agency)* is attempting to collect *(amount of claimed debt).*

I am a victim of identity theft. The debt about which your agency contacted me is the result of fraud by someone who used my personal information without my knowledge or consent. I have enclosed a copy of the police report I filed when I learned of the crime. *(Instead of the police report, the Federal Trade Commission identity theft affidavit can be provided.)* Please provide me with any forms such as a fraud affidavit that your company will require me to fill out to have this account properly investigated as fraud if the enclosed FTC Fraud Affidavit is not sufficient.

I have enclosed the following documents to prove my claim of fraud:

(List copies of any documents you enclose with the letter that prove your claim of identity theft. Such documents could be a copy of a police report, copy of your Federal Trade Commission's Fraud Affidavit, or correspondence between you and a credit bureau, a merchant, or a bank. Lease agreements and utility bills often help prove you were living somewhere other than where the account was established.)

This is to give you notice to cease all contact with me or anyone else about this claimed debt except the creditor or consumer reporting agency as necessary to clear my name. I understand that under state and federal law, you may only contact me one more time in order to confirm your receipt of this request.

In addition, the Fair Debt Collection Practices Act gives me the right to a copy of applications or other documents your agency has obtained as proof of the debt. Please forward copies of any such documents you now have or later obtain to me at the above address.

I look forward to your acknowledgement that you have received this notice by *(date that is two weeks from date of letter)*.

Sincerely,

978-0-595-48128-6
0-595-48128-0